e to return re the

The Well Teacher
promoting staff health, beating stress and reducing absence

Maureen Cooper

Published by Network Educational Press Ltd.
PO Box 635
Stafford
ST16 1BF

First Published 2000
© Maureen Cooper

ISBN 1 85539 058 2

Series Co-ordinator - Anat Arkin
Series Editor - Carol Etherington
Cover design by Neil Hawkins, Devine Design
Internal design and layout by Neil Gordon, Init Publishing
Illustrations by Barking Dog Art

Printed in Great Britain by
Redwood Books, Trowbridge, Wilts.

CONTENTS

INTRODUCTION

"You are very important to us, and we are concerned about your long-term health and well-being." This message is commonly given in the private sector, where senior executives and managers often undergo an annual medical examination or check-up, However, it is a message rarely given in education, where we seem to prefer to spend very large amounts of money (reactively) on sick pay and supply cover, and very small amounts of money on staff well-being and health promotion.

With the average shire county spending in the order of £3-4 million on supply teachers covering sickness absence, the DfEE has recently recognised the importance of this by developing a *Healthy Schools Initiative* and a website: *Wired for Health*. The recent DfEE Circular 4/99 (available on the DfEE website) also indicates that managing sickness absence is becoming a priority issue. A model sickness and absence policy is available on the website www.epm.co.uk

We need a fundamental change in the way that staff health issues are viewed in schools. We have to get rid of the old idea that health promotion is a luxury we cannot afford. It is also important for managers to recognise that the health of staff is part of their responsibility. Failing to check whether the workplace is contributing to an employee's poor health leaves the employer legally vulnerable.

Senior staff in schools need training and support in managing staff absence as, hitherto, there has been little information and advice to help them to develop the necessary skills and knowledge.

This book gives straightforward practical advice on how to deal with staff health issues at the strategic level through the introduction of new school policies and whole-school review, and at the individual level by outlining how to deal with individual cases of staff absence. It addresses the need for a proactive approach to the issue of health management by governors and senior and middle managers.

It also examines the costs, both financial and educational, of staff absence and includes advice on reducing stress levels in schools. A case study based on a sickness absence record illustrates the importance of dealing with staff health issues in a timely and effective way.

This book is intended not only to inform but also to provide a practical point of reference for managers and governors in their day-to-day personnel management. It provides examples of policies and good practice, for example a model of how to record absence patterns. Schools can use these models as templates to be adapted to suit the needs of their working context.

The text makes specific reference to the legal framework that places duties and obligations on governors and managers. There is clear guidance on the difficult issues and procedures inherent in both the dismissal and retirement of teachers because of poor attendance records and ill-health. The final section examines the *Disability Discrimination Act, 1995*, and its implications for staff recruitment.

Maureen Cooper

The following icons are used throughout the book to identify certain types of information:

   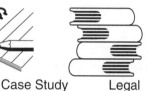

Checklist　　　Model Procedure　　　　　　　　Case Study　　　Legal

CHAPTER 1
EFFECTS ON SCHOOLS OF POOR STAFF HEALTH

Health problems at work cost money. More importantly, poor health of staff in a school will impact on the quality of teaching and learning and so affect pupils' and students' entitlement to education.

Ill-health not only results in impaired performance of individuals; it can also have serious implications for the efficient functioning of a school. Increased and unpredictable sickness absence, a high turnover of staff and lack of energy and enthusiasm for school development are the predictable outcomes of poor health in a school. This can become a downward spiral, where there is increased:

- stress among staff who have to cover for absent colleagues;
- stress among staff who have to make up for the reduced efficiency of stress-impaired colleagues.

Stress is a permanent aspect of life and is not peculiar to the education sector. If its harmful effects are ignored, because it is thought that they are too subjective or too difficult to tackle, then unnecessary ill-health will continue to occur. There is no perfect solution but improvements can be made in almost all work situations. These reflect and depend on good management principles and procedures. A more open and informed attitude to the problems of stress also allows more opportunities for individuals to emerge from the isolation of their own anxieties.

The Industrial Society (*Wish You Were Here,* 1993) established that stress is reported as the second most common cause of absence (after colds and flu). The CBI (*Managing Attendance - in sickness and in health,* 1994) estimates that "stress is the major cause of absence among non-manual workers". Other research has estimated that up to 10% of the workforce experience disabling emotional or physical ill-health related to occupational stress and as many as 30% suffer from a fluctuating array of minor psychological discomforts and physical ailments.

The qualitative evidence available suggests that these general quantitative estimates are very unlikely to overstate the position in education.

The psychological health of employees affects an organisation's capacity to function effectively. Consequently, it is a legitimate matter of concern to management and individual employees.

Furthermore, sickness, absenteeism, reduced productivity and loss of experienced teachers, plus the associated supply teacher and other replacement and recruitment costs, can add up to a significant amount. Therefore, it is often cost-beneficial for the school to be proactive about health promotion. There are also indirect costs related to the decline in the quality of education offered to pupils. Although difficult to quantify, these should be recognised.

Schools spend up to £120 per day to cover teacher absence, though the true cost may well be higher when administrative and other costs such as insurance are taken into account. Making even a modest saving of, say, 10% of a school's supply teacher budget will free up funds which can be used proactively to support staff health. Of course, the use of supply teachers to cover sickness absence is sometimes unavoidable. However, ensuring that it is minimised as far as possible not only creates the opportunity to use resources in a more positive way but also to ensure continuity of teaching and learning for pupils and students.

Absence: a checklist of facts

Absence:

- costs money;
- causes more stress;
- decreases motivation;
- can damage the quality of teaching and learning.

Health promotion:

- can reduce costs;
- increases well-being;
- can reduce absence;
- helps to sustain the quality of teaching and learning.

CHAPTER 2
STAFF HEALTH - THE ROLE OF THE GOVERNORS AND SENIOR MANAGERS

 At common law, the employer has an obligation to take reasonable care of all employees and to guard against reasonable foreseeable risks of injury. These duties are judged in the light of 'the state of the art' knowledge of the employer - either that which was known or ought to have been known.

Employers are also under a statutory duty to ensure, so far as is reasonably practicable, the health, safety and welfare at work of all their employees. Both of these general duties dictate prevention and protection.

Employers are not expected to be prophets, nor are they expected to remain ignorant of the growing knowledge of health and safety matters.

Breach of the common law duty of care exposes the employer to an action for personal injury. Breach of the statutory duty is a criminal offence, punishable by a maximum fine of £20,000 in a magistrate's court or by an unlimited fine on indictment in the Crown Court.

The Management of Health and Safety at Work Regulations 1992 (the Management Regulations) require the employer to carry out a suitable and sufficient assessment of health and safety risks at work. The purpose is to identify the measures which the employer should take to comply with his/her statutory duties, including the general duty to ensure safety. Failing to carry out a risk assessment is also a criminal offence, punishable by a fine of £5,000 in a magistrate's court or by an unlimited fine on indictment in the Crown Court. The Management Regulations also require health surveillance with regard to the risks identified by the risk assessment.

However, if one member of the employer's staff knows about a risk or health or safety problem, then, whether this is shared with the employer or not, the employer is deemed to know about it. This is called constructive knowledge. Ignorance is no defence in law.

When judging whether the employer ought to have acted, the courts will look at the state of knowledge at the time of the alleged act of negligence. Many employers, even those where the risk may seem low such as banks, building societies and transport companies, train their staff to deal with violent customers and offer counselling and support after such incidents.

The legal duty to look after the health, safety and welfare of employees includes a duty to rectify, as far as is reasonable, workloads, workplace events and workplace practices likely to cause ill-health. This includes psychological disturbance such as stress.

A summary of the duties of the employer

1. A duty to take positive steps to ensure the safety of the employee in the light of the knowledge the employer has or ought to have.

2. A right to follow current recognised practice.

3. Where there is developing knowledge, a duty to keep reasonably abreast with it.

4. Where the employer has greater than average knowledge of the risk, a duty to take greater than average precautions.

5. A duty to weigh up the risk, in terms of the likelihood of the injury and the possible consequences, against the cost and inconvenience of precautionary measures.

A positive policy towards health at work, including psychological health, can improve morale and work performance, and lower sickness absence.

There are a number of ways in which management, at all levels, can begin to address 'well-being at work'. The planned implementation of policies to manage staff health issues helps governors and senior managers meet that responsibility.

However, all managers, as well as governors, must first accept that their role encompasses a responsibility for all aspects of managing the performance of staff, including sickness absence and health at work.

Management posts in schools have traditionally focused on the concepts of curriculum management (which implies managing what is taught, not managing the people who teach it) and pastoral management (which means managing pupils, not staff).

The idea that middle or senior managers carry wider responsibility is still unusual in schools, although commonplace in many other fields of employment.

Therefore, if the governors and the headteacher want to promote well-being at work, they must:

- develop an awareness amongst managers of the importance of managing all aspects of an employee's performance at work;
- ensure that these managers have the skills and motivation to promote and manage well-being at work.

Managers' checklist for well-being at work

Managers will need to:
- understand the school's approach to well-being at work;
- know what their responsibilties are and be confident to carry them out;
- communicate effectively between management and team members especially in matters to do with organisational change;
- foster a supportive environment within which stress and health issues can be proactively addressed and the management style is not seen as threatening.

Each school (and local education authority) should analyse its own situation and develop appropriate action plans with the staff involved. Using the strategies outlined will help them do this effectively.

Developing an action plan

Action plans can involve looking at a number of different aspects of the school culture:

- training, induction and career development;
- the classroom situation (workload, resources, relationships with disruptive pupils);
- the physical work environment;
- school organisation (management style, communications);
- external factors (political and community expectations).

CHAPTER 3
DEALING WITH STRESS

Most staff in schools view the job that they do as stimulating and rewarding, and from time to time it may be quite demanding. We are not concerned here with the normal day-to-day demands of a job but those excess pressures that may be a risk to health.

The duty of care

An employer owes a duty of care to employees not to cause them psychiatric damage by the volume or character of the work which they are required to perform.

The law regarding the extent of the duty on an employer to provide the employee with a safe system of work, and to take reasonable steps to protect him or her from risks which are reasonably foreseeable, has developed almost exclusively in cases involving physical injury to an employee.

However, there is no logical reason why risk of injury to an employee's mental health should be excluded from the employer's duty. What is reasonable depends on:

- the nature of the relationship;
- the magnitude of the risk of injury which was reasonably foreseeable;
- the seriousness of the consequences for the person to whom the duty is owed of the risk occurring;
- the practicability of preventing the risk.

Dealing with change

Alongside the stress factors which can be experienced in any organisation, for example poor communication, conflicts with colleagues, unnecessary form-filling and ineffective meetings, staff in education are having to adapt to major changes, both organisational and societal. For some staff, this may conflict with their own ideas of the job they are employed to do.

The case of Walker v Northumberland County Council (1995)

Mr Walker was a senior social worker in charge of four teams of social workers employed by Northumberland County Council. He suffered a nervous breakdown towards the end of 1986. He returned to work in March 1987. He experienced stress again in the summer of 1987 and subsequently suffered another nervous breakdown.

Mr Walker had argued for a restructuring of social services to ease pressure of work before his first nervous breakdown but his suggestions were not adopted. After his first nervous breakdown, Mr Walker was promised support but this did not materialise. The Court found Northumberland County Council not liable for the first breakdown but liable for the second. Amongst the Court's findings were the following:

- Northumberland County Council was not in breach of its duty to take steps to protect Mr Walker from the risk of psychiatric damage prior to his first breakdown. The yardstick was reasonable conduct measured by the relationship of the parties, the magnitude of the risk which was reasonably foreseeable and the seriousness of that injury if it did occur.
- After Mr Walker's first breakdown, Northumberland County Council ought to have foreseen that, if he was again exposed to the same kind of workload, there was a risk that he would suffer another illness.

The Council was ordered to pay damages (reported as £175,000) for his lost career and permanent psychological impairment.

Responses to change

Changes in management arrangements in schools are seen by some staff as a chance to learn and practise new skills; others feel their job description has been radically altered without enough consultation and that they are being asked to perform tasks for which they have not been trained. Increased parental involvement in schools is welcomed by some staff, but is viewed by others as a threat to their position as teachers.

Whatever the merits of such changes, there is no doubt that dealing with change is an aspect of the job that is here to stay and, where it is a source of stress, the consequences need to be positively managed.

It is important to recognise that in some situations the job content, working environment or the personal disposition of an employee can lead to the kind of psychological difficulties which are commonly referred to as stress and which may have physical as well as psychological symptoms.

The fact that an employee is over-stressed should not be seen as an inevitable part of modern life nor as a sign of individual weakness.

Over-stress commonly occurs when there is an unresolved mismatch between the perceived pressures of the work situation and an individual's ability to cope. Health problems, home pressures such as money worries or marital difficulties can reduce the ability to cope with pressures at work.

People's experience of stress at work is affected by:
- the level of control they have over the pressures of work;
- the support they receive from others in meeting those pressures;
- the strategies they use to respond to work pressures.

A medical problem

Psychological health is part of overall personal health and not a separate entity. Stress may be a sign of a more serious medical problem which impairs a person's ability to cope with the pressures of work. It is important, therefore, that an employee who appears to be suffering from stress is encouraged to take medical advice to rule out more serious medical conditions.

Stress may cause symptoms like headaches, indigestion and muscle tension. Over a longer period, it may also contribute to chronic health problems such as raised blood pressure, heart disease and stomach ulcers.

Responses to stress vary, both between individuals and over time; some individuals may primarily experience physical symptoms while others could experience psychological disturbance. The advice here is intended to help identify the early stages of stress when an individual is having difficulty in coping with the pressures of work and ways in which those pressures can be relieved.

Effects on individuals

For the individual, stress can result in a range of unpleasant emotions such as tension, frustration, anxiety and depression. These can lead to lack of interest at work and reduced job satisfaction, which combine to worsen performance. Self-confidence, essential for successful teaching, can be severely eroded and maintaining discipline in the classroom can become increasingly difficult.

Individuals under stress can also show a wide variety of behavioural changes. Colleagues or managers may be able to identify such individuals at an early stage by being aware of some of the changes in normal patterns of behaviour which may suggest increasing stress.

Stress-related changes in behaviour

Work performance	Interpersonal relationships	Personal presentation and behaviour
■ absenteeism;	■ unusual irritability or aggression;	■ changes in appetite;
■ inability to concentrate;	■ becoming withdrawn or unsociable;	■ increasing use of coffee, cigarettes, alcohol or drugs;
■ overworking and failure to delegate;	■ increased resentment of advice or constructive criticism;	■ changes in personal appearance, habit or behaviour.
■ unexpected difficulties with, or resistance to, training;	■ reduced willingness to co-operate.	
■ drop in usual standards of performance;		
■ poor timekeeping.		

Management strategies for dealing with stress at work

Much available advice on stress at work has concentrated on how individuals can be helped to avoid or cope with stress. Less attention has been given to organisational practices that may contribute to stress and how such practices may be altered. This emphasis on the individual has detracted from the role that schools and education authorities play both in contributing to and dealing with stress problems.

Stress problems should be approached from both the organisational and individual levels, with each making an important contribution. Neither strategy on its own is likely to be totally effective.

The first essential element must be that management recognises and communicates that pressure of work can trigger illness, that stress and illness can be related, and that illness through stress does not indicate weakness, incompetence or laziness. Most people suffering from mental ill-health will recover from that illness if treated appropriately.

To work well, any problem-solving process should reflect the commitment of senior managers and the Governing Body to discussing and implementing appropriate changes and an emphasis on preventing stressful situations rather than coping with them. Dealing with stress is a continuing task rather than a one-off process.

Developing plans for identifying and dealing with stressful situations resulting from organisational factors will need to involve all staff. Because teaching, caretaking, etc. involve working in isolation from colleagues for substantial periods each day, an environment that focuses on problems as individual rather than team concerns can increase people's feelings of isolation and helplessness.

Group problem-solving can help to develop co-operation, team spirit and sharing standards and aims; so it needs to be encouraged as a legitimate management practice. It works best in a relaxed and positive atmosphere in which conflict and resistance can be reduced by using an open and exploratory style. Managers will need to consider ways of bringing staff together to discuss problem areas and proposals for change. The emphasis should be on encouraging practical solutions that are proactive not reactive and on prevention and preparing rather than coping.

The perils of ignoring teachers' stress

Since the Walker ruling, a number of teachers have won out-of-court settlements for work-related stress.

In the first of these cases, a technology teacher whose career was ruined by mental illness won over £100,000. His union alleged that he had been bullied by his headteacher and that his local education authority had failed to protect him from foreseeable injury or give him adequate support.

Another high profile case involved a teacher who took ill-health retirement eight years after first complaining about her excessive workload. Claiming that her employer had failed to act on her record of stress-related illness and had done nothing to reduce her 66-hour working week, she accepted a £47,000 out-of-court settlement. As in the earlier case, her employer did not admit liability.

Since neither of these cases came to trial, they did not establish a legal precedent. However, the size of the two settlements is expected to encourage claims from other teachers whose careers have been cut short by stress at work.

Pupil discipline

Teaching is a constant stream of interactions with pupils. When these interactions are co-operative and courteous, then stress levels are, for most teachers, maintained at appropriate levels. The greater the number of adversarial interactions, the more likely it is that the teacher will become over-stressed.

The school behaviour policy is therefore vitally important in the management of stress.

A checklist for the management of pupil discipline

- Is there a whole-school behaviour policy setting out expected standards of behaviour?
- Is it available to, and understood by, all staff, pupils, parents and governors?
- Are senior and middle managers supportive when dealing with discipline problems?
- Do managers make time to discuss strategies for dealing with specific discipline problems?
- Are staff encouraged to discuss discipline problems and agree team strategies to promote team spirit and reduce the sense of isolation?
- Is there adequate staff participation in development or change of the discipline policy and behaviour management training?
- Does induction and in-service training provide adequate opportunity to discuss stressful situations arising from discipline problems?
- Are job descriptions clear about the extent of individual responsibilities?
- Does the school take action to encourage a positive perception of its discipline standards by parents and the general community?
- In what ways are staff, pupils and the community encouraged to show respect for the school environment and the people in it?
- Is there effective feedback on staff performance after dealing with disruptive pupils?

By systematically considering aspects of school tasks, which, if not well managed, can lead to stress, staff should be able to identify changes, whether minor or major, that will both improve the quality of management and be beneficial to individuals.

Developing a supportive culture

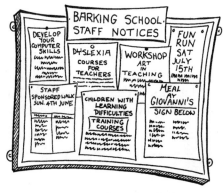

To create the right environment for staff to talk openly to each other about problems, managers should look at ways of enhancing social support or developing a 'caring culture' within the school.

By encouraging peer groups, supervisors and subordinates to talk and socialise together, a spirit of co-operation and camaraderie can be developed to help to overcome feelings of isolation in the classroom.

Recognising stress problems through information and training

Everybody involved in group problem-solving and improvement of the caring culture will need access to some information and training on stress if problems are to be identified and dealt with effectively.

Consultants, occupational health staff and health education counsellors can advise on and assist with appropriate training schemes. Information on stress at work is plentiful. Some references for further general reading are given in Appendix E.

A checklist of how managers can support staff

Strategies for senior managers include:

- ensuring they are accessible to staff to discuss problems and anxieties;
- taking a lead in changing the view that being under stress is a reflection of personal vulnerability;
- devising effective induction programmes for new staff;
- encouraging staff to talk about pressure points in the job;
- encouraging, commending and recognising supportive behaviour in others;
- developing co-operative rather than competitive management styles;
- engendering team spirit, a sense of belonging and the sharing of aims and objectives;
- recognising individuals' fears of return to work after sickness absence and providing support;
- encouraging staff to make use of occupational health advice.

Identifying pressure points

The use of an anonymous questionnaire will help managers to identify the main pressure points during the school day, term and year. Pressure points might occur in relation to a department or to physical areas of the school, or to the distribution of work during the school year.

Pressure points questionnaire

	Agree very strongly	Agree	Neither agree nor disagree	Disagree	Disagree very strongly
The area that I work in helps to make my work pleasant and productive.					
I have enough teaching resources.					
The quality of teaching resources available to me is adequate for my needs.					
I believe that my workload is appropriate to the job that I am paid to do.					
The tasks that I am asked to do are appropriate to my job description.					
Parents evenings are well organised by management.					
Staff/department/team meetings are worthwhile.					
I understand my role in pupil discipline.					
Senior staff are supportive in pupil discipline.					
I feel that I am in control of my work.					
There are often conflicting demands during my working time.					
Pressure builds up during the course of each term.					
I always feel refreshed and ready to begin a new term.					
The behaviour policy works well.					
The duty system works well.					

Personal strategies for dealing with stress at work

People have different 'stress' thresholds. A situation perceived as threatening by one person may be seen as challenging or of no significance by another.

A self-help checklist

- Knowing in some depth what causes stress for you, recognising the symptoms early and having strategies to deal with it are key features of managing stress.
- You are your most important ally.
- Good health, including eating sensibly, getting enough rest and avoiding the harmful effects of alcohol and tobacco is important.
- Taking regular exercise such as walking, swimming or cycling is beneficial.
- Make time for yourself to enjoy leisure activities and interests.
- Talking things through with friends and relatives is helpful. If problems become too much, talking to a counsellor may help.
- Giving yourself thinking time each day can help you to manage your time and priorities.
- Rest and relaxation are crucial. Learning to relax and taking at least one break during the day will help to sustain you.

Ways of coping

- Define the problem by obtaining all relevant information, considering alternative approaches to deal with it and establishing goals.

- Does stress arise because your own expectations of yourself and/or others are not met? If so, recognising and modifying unrealistic expectations, establishing attainable goals, accepting your own limitations and avoiding inappropriate over-involvement may help.

- Does a particular occasion/event always prove stressful? In this case, 'anticipatory coping' (e.g. preparation, planning, mental rehearsal) will help.

- Is workload management a problem? Consider coping strategies such as setting priorities, delegation, time-management, recognition that some workload is self-imposed, being realistic about how much can be done, forward planning and anticipating and regulating demands.

- If an acute conflict arises, a 'cooling-off' period may be a helpful short-term measure.

- Self-monitoring whilst under stress, and learning to recognise unhelpful and self-defeating responses, reduce vulnerability.

- Seek the support of others, particularly senior colleagues.

Four key areas of self-help

Relaxation

Learn to recognise the onset of tension and take action to alleviate it. Health Education Authority centres, local libraries or community groups may be able to provide information about courses on relaxation techniques. Books and audio tapes intended for home use are available. Examples of techniques include deep muscle relaxation, meditation, breathing exercises and yoga.

Diet and exercise

Lack of physical fitness makes mental fitness harder to achieve. Physical exercise can also help to reduce tension and enhance mood. Regular exercise and sensible diet increase fitness and self-esteem as well as resilience to stress.

Interpersonal skills

Sometimes, people bring stress on themselves by the way in which they deal with others. Personality analysis and training in communication skills such as assertiveness may be helpful.

Social support

Building and maintaining a supportive network of family, friends and colleagues with whom you can share problems is an effective sponge for helping to absorb the adverse effects of stress at work.

How managers should act

Management of health issues, especially work-related stress, is an important aspect of a manager's role. If all staff who have a line management responsibility for others improved their practice in the following three areas, then the organisational benefits would be considerable:

- ensuring that they communicate effectively with their own line manager(s) on the issues listed below;
- being aware of their own motivation/resilience levels and having self-help strategies available to use when levels are low;
- seeking help from their own line manager(s) when those strategies fail.

A checklist for managers

When dealing with your staff:

1. Take care over the allocation of work, in particular when planning the timetable for teaching colleagues.

2. Keep jobs under review to ensure that no-one has an unbalanced workload. If there is overload, then do what you can to address that (without taking on too much more yourself).

3. Meet all employees reporting to you on a planned and regular basis. Provide opportunities to listen to their concerns. Listen, and where appropriate, act on what they have to say.

4. Be proactive about absence management, following the school's absence policy.

5. Be proactive about the induction of new employees.

6. Be aware that changed job requirements are a significant cause of stress. Ensure that colleagues who are affected are supported and monitored accordingly.

7. Identify the training and development needs of your staff and make arrangements to monitor progress in meeting those needs.

8. Be aware of the fluctuating motivation/resilience levels of staff and have strategies available to 'step in' when levels are low.

9. Be aware of what causes major increases in stress for staff and when that is likely to occur. Develop strategies accordingly.

CHAPTER 4
HEALTH PROMOTION

An occupational health service for the school

Local Authority employers usually have an occupational health service, though very often schools are unaware of the range and type of services provided, or indeed the cost of the service. The arrival of Fair Funding should mean that schools will know how much the LEA occupational health service is costing them. Heads and governors will then be able to decide whether they would rather have the money so that the school can make its own local arrangements, either individually or in a group with other schools.

The LEA does, however, have the responsibility for checking the health of new employees, and has to retain the services of a medical adviser for that purpose. Foundation and aided schools (who are, of course, the employers of staff) need to decide on their arrangements for checking employees on appointment and whether or not they wish to develop an occupational health scheme.

Small firms sometimes become members of a group occupational health service. This could be developed by a group of schools on a shared basis. Normally, this is based on an annual per capita subscription, though most services will operate on a fee for service basis if required. Each member school could expect to receive regular visits from an experienced nurse who is available for consultation by employees. The visiting nurse could provide basic health screening and perhaps provide first-aid training.

Occupational health should be concerned with preventing ill-health and promoting health and well-being in the workplace. Occupational health professionals, such as psychologists, nurses and doctors, can increase awareness of self-help strategies for employees by leading training sessions and discussion groups and promoting a supportive culture. Similarly, they can advise on positive health management, including diet, exercise, drugs, drinking and smoking.

Ideally, staff should have the opportunity to seek advice from occupational health personnel, who will discuss problems in confidence and, where necessary, initiate appropriate advice on treatment through the employee's doctor. Such a scheme enables staff to access trained health professionals who can, if necessary, refer to other specialist advice such as coping-skills training, group therapy and psychological treatment.

Employing a nurse

A qualified occupational health nurse (that is a registered nurse with an occupational health nursing certificate) can provide a very good basic service by:

- monitoring causes and levels of sickness absence;
- providing health education and other counselling;
- supervising and training first aiders;
- providing regular health checks;
- consulting other occupational health specialists if necessary.

Pre-employment health screening

A Local Education Authority or Governing Body must not appoint anyone to a teaching post or continue to employ them as a teacher unless s/he has the health and physical capacity for such employment (Regulations 8 and 9 of the Teachers Regulations). This includes an agency or supply teacher, or other person working with children and young persons under 19, at schools maintained by local education authorities. In making decisions about medical fitness, employers must adhere to the provisions of the Disability Discrimination Act, 1995. Guidance is available from organisations such as the Employment Service Disability Service.

DfEE Circular No: 4/99 *Physical and Mental Fitness to Teach of Teachers and of Entrants to Initial Teacher Training* says that all employers of teachers should take advice from a medical adviser acting for the employer.

The circular also says that, if the medical adviser to the prospective employer considers that a specialist opinion is necessary, the applicant may be offered the opportunity to choose a specialist on the advice of their GP, or the medical adviser may propose a specialist with the agreement of the applicant. An applicant who does not agree with the recommendation of the prospective employer's medical adviser may seek another specialist's opinion, again guided by his or her GP. The employer's medical adviser should consider, in the light of any such second opinion, whether his or her previous advice should be revised. The decision on whether to accept such an applicant rests with the employer.

 The principle at common law is that you take your victim as you find him. This was well illustrated in the case (not involving an employer) of *Page v Smith* (House of Lords, *The Times*, 1 May 1994). Here, a negligent motorist was held liable for the victim's nervous shock and for his chronic fatigue syndrome which he had had in a mild form but which, he argued had been exacerbated by the accident. The House of Lords held that chronic fatigue syndrome existed, that a relapse or worsening of the condition could be triggered by the trauma of an accident, and that nervous shock was suffered by the plaintiff who was actually involved in the accident. It became a foreseeable consequence.

If liability had been established for nervous shock, the defendant would have been liable for all the consequent mental injury sustained by the victim even though it was unforeseen and of a kind that would only be suffered by someone who was particularly vulnerable. The judge said that it was well established that the defendant must in law take the plaintiff as he found him.

It is essential that suitable and relevant questions are addressed on the pre-employment medical questionnaire so that relevant and adequate information is gathered.

CHAPTER 5
EFFECTIVE TECHNIQUES FOR MANAGING SICKNESS ABSENCE

 These guidelines are written in accordance with the Access to Medical Reports Act, 1988 and the Disability Discrimination Act, 1995. This legislation applies to any situation where an employee has had clinical care or has a disability. Clinical care is defined as: "Examination, investigation or diagnosis for the purpose of, or in connection with, any form of medical treatment." Disability is defined as: "A physical or mental impairment which has a substantial or long-term adverse effect on their ability to carry out normal day-to-day activities".

The nature of ill-health problems means that each case will be different. Headteachers should take personnel advice about the management of each specific case. In a case of genuine ill-health, as distinct from a case of misconduct or lack of capability to carry out the post, the employee cannot improve his/her performance or conduct by his/her own efforts. Understanding, care and skilful management are needed in order to be fair to the employee and to protect the school's good name as an employer from claims of unfair dismissal to an Employment Tribunal. The school must also act in accordance with the Disability Discrimination Act. It is good practice to have a policy of return to work interviews, irrespective of the length of absence. This makes it caring rather than threatening.

The steps in dealing with sickness absence

The length of time taken to follow the steps set out below will vary considerably from one case to another. However, as a rule of thumb, it is wise to begin to consult an employee sooner rather than later and to consider using the benchmark of seven days absence as a starting point for consultation. At this stage, consultation could be the responsibility of the line manager, though this will have training implications for middle management in many schools.

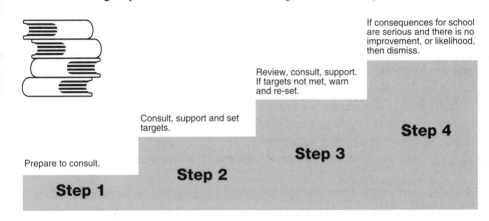

If consequences for school are serious and there is no improvement, or likelihood, then dismiss.

Review, consult, support. If targets not met, warn and re-set.

Consult, support and set targets.

Prepare to consult.

Step 1
Step 2
Step 3
Step 4

Step 1.   Prepare to consult the employee

- Refer to the school's statistical data on levels and types of sickness for all staff. (See Chapter 6 on how to record sickness absence).
- Establish that the member of staff causing concern has a higher than 'average' level of absence or that the record shows a pattern of absence or some other factual data which identifies the cause for concern.
- Identify the nature of the absence.
- Establish the employee's age and length of service at the school; the longer the service, the less hasty the dismissal.
- Consider the job description and the implications of the absences to the work of the school and to the work group, i.e. the more serious the implications, the more pressing and severe the remedy.
- If it is possible that the meeting might result in the employee being told that dismissal may be considered (i.e. Step 3 has been reached) unless the attendance record improves, then the employee should be informed in writing beforehand of his/her right to be accompanied by a trade union representative or a friend. It is, however, often helpful to allow employees to be accompanied at earlier stages since it helps to leave no doubt about the nature of the problem and the expected improvement.

Step 2.   Consult and support the employee

The employee should be consulted and the matter thoroughly discussed. Consultation, with the headteacher, the line manager or other appropriate person, will often bring to light facts and circumstances of which the headteacher was unaware and which will throw new light on the problem. Aim to gather enough information about the nature of the problem to enable the employer to make a realistic assessment of the situation and consider the appropriate response. It is very important that steps are taken to discover the true medical position.

If the school conducts return to work interviews as a matter of course, then expressing concern will be seen as part of a continuum rather than a sudden and threatening intervention by management.

It is important that employees are advised sooner rather than later that the level of sickness absence is causing concern and that it must be reduced because of the effect that the level of absence is having on the organisation. Try to be very specific, e.g. quantify the percentage of lessons lost because of absence.

If a sickness absence problem has been ignored until everyone is exasperated, then the school has two problems: the sickness absence problem and the failure of management to deal with it. It is important that the employer investigates carefully any suggestion that the employee makes that the workload or working conditions are contributing to the absence record. Any reasonable adjustments that can be made should be made.

Where the employee recognises that there is little prospect of improvement, s/he may be willing to consider a less arduous post or a move to part-time. Employees should never be badgered into such decisions. If the employee volunteers, having had the opportunity to take advice, then the employer should not unreasonably refuse to offer the alternative employment, if it is available.

It is important that the employee is given a reasonable amount of time in which to improve his/her attendance record. This might be one term, but what is reasonable will vary from case to case, particularly in relation to the importance of the job and the functioning of the school. Targets should be set, identifying:

- the level of improvement required;
- the period over which improvement must be achieved.

Step 2 should be repeated at least once and probably more than once. A written record should be kept of each interview, and a copy provided for the employee and representative.

Step 3.   Review, consult, support and warn the employee

If the employee was not asked to see the school's medical adviser as part of Step 1, then this must happen at Step 2. The employee is entitled to refuse consent to a medical examination by the school's medical adviser, but if s/he does then the employer would be justified in continuing to deal with the matter since reasonable efforts had been made to establish the true medical position. The nearer the employer moves to Step 4, the more important it is that the employee is warned that dismissal is a possibility.

The employee should be warned about the likely consequence of a failure to improve. It must be spelled out and confirmed in writing so that there is no possibility that the employee may say that s/he did not understand.

Step 4.   Dismissal on the grounds of ill-health

A checklist of questions to answer before a dismissal

Consider the following:

- How long has the employee been employed? The longer the service, the less hasty the employer should be to dismiss.
- Has the impact on the school been objectively identified as so serious that the employer cannot be expected to wait any longer for the employee to recover and/or return to normal working?
- Is the employee incapacitated by industrial injury through no fault of his/her own and therefore deserving some special treatment?
- Is there a possible danger to pupils, to fellow employees or other adults with whom the employee would come into contact on his/her return to work?
- Have other persons with relevant information been consulted?
- Is the work of other employees seriously disrupted by his/her absence or incapacity?
- Has the employee been properly consulted and offered the opportunity to be represented?

31

- Has medical evidence been sought?
- Have adjustments to the job been considered?
- Has a reasonable search for alternative work been made?
- Is ill-health dismissal fair?

If there is no improvement, or likelihood of improvement, then there may no reasonable alternative but to dismiss the employee.

The employer should have regard to the sick pay entitlement of the employee. If the employee is entitled to, for example, six months full pay and six months half pay and the employer moves to dismissal before the full pay entitlement is exhausted, then a tribunal may regard the action as too hasty.

An employee should never be dismissed on the basis of medical evidence alone. It is very important to establish the impact of the employee's absence on the organisation.

If it is necessary to dismiss the employee, the consideration of dismissal must be carried out by the committee of governors which has delegated power to dismiss. The employee has the right of appeal against dismissal to the appeals committee of the governors.

Employees will sometimes apply for an ill-health retirement pension when they realise that the employer is minded to dismiss. Sometimes, employees indicate that they intend to do this in the hope that the employer will stop pursuing the poor attendance record. Employers should bear in mind that the decision to apply for the pension is a matter for the employee and there is no guarantee that it will be granted.

It is important to distinguish between different categories of absence through ill health:

- persistent short-term absences for unconnected medical reasons;
- long-term sickness or persistent short-term absences due to a single cause or related causes;
- persistent short-term absences and there is evidence to suggest that the person is capable of work on those days.

Persistent short-term absences caused by unconnected illnesses

Where the employee appears to suffer a series of unconnected ailments, s/he should be asked to consent to a medical examination by the school's medical adviser. If it is established that improvement is unlikely, then a point may be reached where the employer is entitled to say 'enough is enough' and will be justified in treating the persistent absences as a sufficient reason for dismissal.

In this case, the headteacher should be satisfied that the absence is excessive in comparison with other employees carrying out the same or similar types of work, with the result that the contribution is considered inadequate or excessively disruptive to the day-to-day running of the school.

Long-term sickness or persistent short-term absences due to a single cause or related causes

Employment tribunals generally take the view that there should be a discussion to weigh up the situation. This discussion should bear in mind the employer's need for work to be done and the employee's need for time in which to recover his/her health.

These categories refer to employees whose ill-health is connected with an underlying complaint, e.g. heart, chest, or back, which causes long-term or intermittent absences, or poor performance. The employer should try to establish whether the employee is:

a. absent sick and unable to return to work at all;
b. absent sick but able to return to less arduous duties;
c. absent sick for a long period and there is doubt about whether and when a return to work is possible;
d. frequently absent sick to such an extent that his/her contribution is considered inadequate, or the work, and/or that of others, is seriously disrupted.

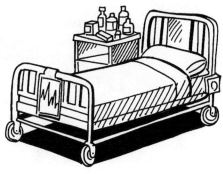

If the absent employee is unable to attend for interview at the place of work or some other convenient place, it may be appropriate to ask whether he/she can be visited at home or in hospital. If the employee is too sick to be interviewed, or wishes not to be interviewed for other reasons, the situation can, with his/her agreement, be discussed with a third party, e.g. their trade union representative, a close relative or a friend.

The matter for consideration is in no way related to misconduct by the employee, and s/he should not be made to feel that s/he is being reprimanded as a result of incapacity. However, the employee should be left in no doubt that fitness for future employment is under consideration, and that s/he is being consulted about it. Alternative work can be discussed if appropriate.

Seek personnel advice before this course of action is taken and take particular care to avoid placing stress on the individual, especially where the absence is through mental or stress-related illness. If there is no improvement in the employee's fitness (see Step 3), it may be necessary to notify the employee formally that his/her employment is at risk due to ill-health. The employee should be informed beforehand of their right to be accompanied by a trade union representative or a friend at any interview where a formal notification may be made.

Although such 'warnings' may seem inappropriate in cases involving absences due to illness, given that such absences may lead to the loss of a job, they are a necessary measure of fairness for the employee. The individual should be treated with understanding and compassion. Consider whether the employee is suffering from a disability under the terms of the Disability Discrimination Act 1995. It may be unlawful to dismiss by reason of the disability in circumstances where a reasonable job/role adjustment would have prevented the dismissal.

A checklist of possible strategies

Managers should consider the following, depending on the nature of the problem:

- allow the employee to remain absent until s/he can resume work;
- allow the employee to continue in his/her present job, modified if appropriate;
- decide to review the situation after a further specified period;
- agree with the employee a transfer to another job;
- dismiss on grounds of incapability due to ill-health, of no prospect of making a reasonable adjustment, and a lack of alternative employment.

The governors are not obliged to create an alternative job, but they must ensure that a thorough search is made to find a job suitable for an employee who would otherwise be dismissed. It may be reasonable to modify a particular job to make it suitable for such an employee. In considering alternative work, take into account the advice of the school's medical adviser.

Keep a written record of each interview, and provide a copy for the employee and his/her representative.

Absences falsely claimed as sickness

If it is believed that an employee is taking time off sick and is really fit for work, then the headteacher should investigate the matter, normally when the employee returns to work.

The reason for the doubt should be tactfully explained to the employee, who should be invited to offer an explanation. If the explanation is not accepted, then the matter should be regarded as misconduct and dealt with under the school's disciplinary procedures. Another handbook in this series, *Managing Challenging People*, gives advice on how to tackle this.

CHAPTER 6
MONITORING STAFF SICKNESS ABSENCE

The Local Government Management Board (LGMB) conducted a survey of sickness absence amongst school teachers for the school year 1997/98 (the first of its kind).

It showed that the mean absence rate for teachers was 3.64%, or 7.1 days per teacher. LGMB reported that rates were higher for teachers in special schools (5.06%) than those in primary schools (3.65%) or secondary schools (3.54%). Supply cover can cost around £1000 per teacher per school year.

The report indicated that there was significant, if not substantial, variation amongst absence rates recorded by LEAs and concluded that there is scope for some schools and LEAs to learn from others who appear to be managing sickness absence effectively.

Keeping teacher absence records

- Keep a record of each absence by category (single or repeated cause, or one-off).
- Keep a record of each absence by reason, e.g. stomach upset.
- Record other absences separately, e.g. children sick, car would not start, time off for interviews.
- Look at the total absence record and work out the impact on pupils in particular, and the school in general.

- Compare the absence with the rest of the same category of staff.
- Reach a fair and considered view on the impact of the absence on the continuity and quality of teaching and learning provided for the pupils.

All schools should have a clear written policy for handling staff sickness absence and for taking decisive action to reduce levels of absence which disrupt children's education. The policy should include clear procedures, drawn up in consultation with staff, for the careful monitoring of staff absences, for taking appropriate responsive action, and for promoting good health.

Monitoring sickness and absence

The essential features of a sickness absence monitoring procedure are:

- clear guidelines for reporting absence on the first day of absence and beyond;
- frequent contact with absent staff and, on each occasion, agreement on the date and form of next contact;
- records of the number of absences and the working time lost for each spell of absence for each member of staff;
- return to work interviews after each spell of absence, setting clear guidelines about the conduct and content of such interviews and making a record of actions agreed;
- trigger points for management action based on an individual's cumulative absence;
- clear guidance on the range of management actions available;
- clear guidelines for referrals to the school's medical adviser.

The absence record

Mr MacGaw is a (fictitious!) secondary school mathematics teacher. His absence record from October 1997 to July 1999 is set out below.

Autumn Term 1997

09.10.1997 - 10.10.1997	2.0	Self-certificated	Diarrhoea & headache
06.11.1997 - 07.11.1997	2.0	Self-certificated	Cold & asthma
10.12.1997 - 17.12.1997	6.0	Self-certificated	Flu infection

Spring Term 1998

12.01.1998 - 02.02.1998	15.0	Medical certificate	Chest infection
23.02.1998 - 23.02.1998	1.0	Self-certificated	Migraine
16.03.1998 - 03.04.1998	15.0	Unpaid leave	Local election candidate

Summer Term 1998

05.05.1998 - 07.05.1998	3.0	Other	In-service training
15/06/1998 - 19/06/1998	5.0	Self-certificated	Headache, dizziness, nausea
06.07.1998 - 07.07.1998	2.0	Self-certificated	Asthma
24.07.1998 - 24.07.1998	1.0	Other	Moving house

Autumn Term 1998

15.09.1998 - 17.09.1998	3.0	Self-certificated	Asthma
09.11.1998 - 13.11.1998	5.0	Self-certificated	Kidney infection
30.11.1998 - 2.12.1998	3.0	Self-certificated	Asthma
04.12.1998 - 04.12.1998	1.0	Self-certificated	Asthma
07.12.1998 - 07.12.1998	1.0	Other	Dentist
15.12.1998 - 15.12.1998	1.0	Other	Minor car accident
17.12.1998 - 18.12.1998	2.0	Self-certificated	Diarrhoea

Spring Term 1999

11.01.1999 - 13.01.1999	3.0	Self-certificated	Chest cold & asthma
15.01.1999 - 15.01.1999	1.0	Other	Car breakdown
18.01.1999 - 20.01.1999	3.0	Self-certificated	Urinary tract infection
01.02.1999 - 26.02.1999	13.0	Medical certificate	Bronchitis
15.03.1999 - 19.03.1999	5.0	Self-certficated	Stomach & chest pains
22.03.1999 - 23.03.1999	2.0	Self-certificated	Diarrhoea

Summer Term 1999

17.05.1999 - 17.05.1999	1.0	Self-certificated	Sprained ankle
02.06.1999 - 02.06.1999	1.0	Self-certificated	Ear infection
11.06.1999 - 11.06.1999	1.0	Self-certificated	Asthma
23.06.1999 - 25.06.1999	3.0	Self-certificated	Severe headache & sickness
12.07.1999 - 12.07.1999	1.0	Self-certificated	Diarrhoea

Handling Mr MacGaw's absence

Autumn Term 1997
By the end of the Autumn Term 1997, Mr MacGaw had been absent for 10 days. The Autumn Term was 71 days, so his students had substitute teachers for 14% of the maths lessons timetabled for Mr MacGaw. Each of the absences was self-certificated (the Teachers' Conditions of Service require a medical certificate from the sixth working day or the eighth calender day of absence) so Mr MacGaw may not have visited his doctor at all!

At this point, Mr MacGaw should have been interviewed by his line manager or a senior member of staff and had the effect of his absences on the continuity of teaching and learning for his students pointed out to him. The school's expectations should have been made clear to him. He should have been sent a memorandum of the meeting so that there was no room for doubt about the impact of his absence on the school and no doubt that the school wished to support his well-being in whatever way it could reasonably do so.

Spring Term 1998
A pattern of chest-related illness is emerging. On return from the 15-day absence in January, he should have been asked to see the school's medical adviser to see whether this was likely to be an ongoing problem and whether or not there was anything the school could do to help. Mr MacGaw can refuse to see the medical adviser. However, by offering him the opportunity to do so, the school has clearly made reasonable efforts to identify the problem and see if anything can be done to help.

Mr MacGaw is entitled to unpaid leave of absence to be a candidate for the local elections. This is covered by legislation. However, Mr MacGaw was absent for 31 days out of 67 - 46% absence - in the Spring Term. The impact of his absence should have been pointed out to him, together with an indication of the expected level of attendance necessary to ensure continuity of teaching and learning for his students.

Summer Term 1998

Mr MacGaw has three days in-service training. Obviously, this is quite separate from his sickness absence record and a legitimate absence authorised by the school. The school would be unwise to deny Mr MacGaw in-service training opportunities because of his sickness absence record. However, looked at from the students' viewpoint, it does not matter very much to them (or their parents) why their teacher is absent. They just know that they are missing yet more maths lessons with their teacher when their friends do not have to put up with this problem. Mr MacGaw is off for a further five days - again self-certificated - with 'headache, dizziness and nausea'.

This seems, along with the chest problems, to be another recurring problem since he has already had three days off for similar reasons during this academic year. So, a further referral to the medical adviser could be arranged for this new reason.

A Summary of the Academic Year 1997-1998

Type of absence	Sickness absence	Other absence	Total absence
No of days	33 days	19 days	52 days
% of 195 days absent	17%	9 %	26%
Possible supply teacher cost @ £120 day	£3960	£480 (15 unpaid, 4 paid)	£4440
Likely cost to colleagues	Frustration? Loss of non-contact time? Extra work? Increased stress?		
Cost to students	Frustration, leading to complaints or poor behaviour? Loss of entitlement? Poor grades?		

Also, Mr MacGaw could be asked to visit his doctor to provide a medical certificate for all sickness absences so that the school can be sure that he is receiving proper medical advice. After all, he might only have been to the doctor twice since the previous October, even though he has had a total of 33 days absence on seven separate occasions. If the doctor made a charge for these certificates, then the school would have to pay. Ideally, the school will have a statement in its Sickness Absence Management Policy indicating that the headteacher may, where there is concern about the level of sickness, ask for a medical certificate for all sickness absences.

Mr MacGaw completes the academic year by having the last day of the summer term off to move house. Presumably, the school authorised it and should have enquired why it was not possible for the move to take place the following week in the summer break. The headteacher has the right to refuse a request for leave of absence which s/he believes to be unreasonable. If the day was taken without prior agreement, then it should be investigated as a disciplinary matter.

The New Academic Year 1998 -1999
At the beginning of the new term, Mr MacGaw should have been invited to a meeting to discuss the previous year and the coming year. This could have been a formal meeting at which he was offered the opportunity to be accompanied by a trade union representative. The meeting might have resulted in Mr MacGaw being warned that his record of the previous year was unsatisfactory and what improvements are expected in the coming year.

A Summary of the Academic Year 1998-1999

Type of absence	Sickness absence	Other absence	Total absence
No of days	46 days	4 days	50 days
% of 195 days absent	23.5%	2 %	25.5%
Possible supply teacher cost @ £120 day	£5520	£480	£6000
Likely cost to colleagues	Parental complaints? Loss of confidence in senior management? Demoralised maths department?		

However, it looks as though no action of any kind was taken since the serious level of absence continues. So, there may be two problems: Mr MacGaw's absence record and the failure of management to take effective action! Very often, in cases where the absence record is as serious as Mr MacGaw's, there is the additional problem of poor performance. This should be dealt with separately under the school's disciplinary procedures, explained in another handbook in this series, Managing Poor Performance.

Emergency action, suspension or dismissal in relation to medical incapability

A Governing Body or headteacher must take emergency action when they consider a teacher may have become medically incapable of performing teaching duties if this may put at risk the health, education, safety or welfare of pupils. Employers have the wider remit of considering whether a teacher in relevant employment has become medically unfit to perform teaching duties (irrespective of whether emergency action has been taken by a school).

Governing Bodies and headteachers of maintained schools with delegated budgets have powers to suspend teachers where necessary. Several medical conditions may lead to the suspension of a teacher from duty but suspension should only be carried out on the advice of an appropriately qualified medical adviser. The suspension may only be lifted by the Governing Body.

Where the issue of dismissal of a teacher on medical grounds arises, under regulation 9 of the Teachers Regulations, the employer must give that teacher the opportunity to submit medical and other evidence and to make representations, and must consider such evidence and representations. The employee should be asked to give his/her consent to medical evidence being obtained. The employer cannot require an employee to consent to being examined by the LEA's medical adviser or to his/her GP being consulted. However, provided the headteacher has explained the situation clearly and given the employee reasonable opportunity to take advice and consider his/her response, the headteacher is entitled to make a decision without further medical evidence. The situation should be very carefully recorded in writing for both parties.

If the teacher requests a medical examination, then the employer must arrange it. The teacher's own medical adviser may, on request, be present at the examination.

On receipt of the medical advice, the headteacher should consider what to do in the light of it. S/he should not try to judge the soundness of the medical opinion or make a decision solely on the basis of the medical advice. The decision is a managerial one, made in the light of the medical evidence and the other criteria such as are set out above.

Barring - the Secretary of State's powers

The Secretary of State has a discretionary power to make a Direction barring a person from 'relevant employment' or imposing restrictions on a person's employment on medical grounds (Regulation 10 of the Teachers Regulations). A Direction has the force of law and takes effect immediately it is made. It remains in force until it is withdrawn by the Secretary of State. It applies to employers, as well as the person barred, but its effect is confined to relevant employment.

Broadly speaking, barring will only be considered in cases where a person is suffering from an illness that implies a risk or potential risk to the safety and welfare of pupils and colleagues. It is most likely to be considered for a person suffering from mental illness, who has displayed psychotic or manic symptoms, and in cases of severe alcohol or drug misuse.

Teaching staff sickness absence entitlements

The payment of allowances to teachers during periods of absence from duty owing to personal illness, injury or other disability is governed by the terms and conditions set out in the *Conditions of Service for School Teachers in England and Wales* (the Burgundy Book.) Subject to the provisions of this scheme, a teacher (full-time or part-time) is entitled to receive in any period of one year an allowance in accordance with the following scale:

During the first year of service	full pay for 25 working days and after completing four calendar months' service, half pay for 50 working days
During the second year of service	full pay for 50 working days and half pay for 50 working days
During the third year of service	full pay for 75 working days and half pay for 75 working days
During the fourth and successive years	full pay for 100 working days and half pay for 100 working days

'Working days' refers to the 195 days on which a teacher is required to work in accordance with the School Teachers' Pay and Conditions Document. The Governing Body has discretion to extend sick pay in any individual case.

Support staff sickness absence entitlements

Sickness allowances are paid subject to the employee fulfilling certain conditions and obligations. The allowance schemes are intended to secure that, during periods of sickness absence, the employees receive from the sickness allowance and statutory sick pay (or National Insurance benefit) no more than the sum of their normal earnings.

Sickness allowances are paid for the following period:

During the first year of service	1 month full pay plus (after 4 months service) 2 months half pay
During the second year of service	2 months full pay plus 2 months half pay
During the third year of service	4 months full pay plus 4 months half pay
During the fourth/fifth years of service	5 months full pay plus 5 months half pay
After the fifth year of service	6 months full pay plus 6 months half pay

CHAPTER 7
RETIREMENT ON GROUNDS OF ILL-HEALTH

Teachers who are unable to continue work because of illness or injury can apply for ill-health retirement benefits under the Teachers Pension Scheme if they are members of the scheme. A teacher must be permanently unfit to teach to qualify for ill-health benefits.

A checklist of ill-health benefits for employees

An employee who contributes to the Local Government Superannuation Scheme, and who is retired on grounds of ill-health, is eligible to receive the following benefits:

- less than one year's pensionable service - a refund of contributions;

- one or more but less than two years' pensionable service - a one-off lump sum payment known as an ill-health retirement grant;

- two or more, but less than five years' pensionable service, and the school's medical adviser has signed a certificate of permanent ill-health on the employee's behalf - an immediate retirement pension and lump sum;

- five or more years' pensionable service and the school's medical adviser has signed a certificate of permanent ill-health on the employee's behalf - an immediate enhanced retirement pension and an enhanced lump sum.

A team of medical advisers appointed by the DfEE considers applications for ill-health benefit. The DfEE tells the employer of the decision at the same time as the teacher. Teachers may not be re-employed in community, aided or foundation schools whilst in receipt of ill-health benefits granted after 31 March 1997. If such a teacher is appointed, then the ill-health retirement pension would cease immediately. If the ill-health retirement benefits of a teacher became payable before 31 March 1997, s/he may be re-employed on a limited part-time basis. However, the pensions may be subject to abatement and the re-employment will be monitored by the Teachers' Pension Agency (TPA).

A checklist of benefits under the Teachers' Pension Scheme

A teacher who contributes to the Teachers' Pension Scheme and who is retired on grounds of ill-health is eligible to receive the following benefits:

- two to five years' pensionable service - actual pensionable service;
- five to ten years - *double actual pensionable service;
- ten to 13.33 years' pensionable service - 20* years;
- More than 13.33 years' pensionable service - either 20* years OR actual pensionable service plus 6 years 243 days, whichever is more favourable**.

    * this amount cannot be more than the teacher could have achieved by age 65.

    ** this amount cannot be more than the teacher could have achieved by age 60.

CHAPTER 8
THE DISABILITY DISCRIMINATION ACT, 1995

The Disability Discrimination Act (DDA) 1995 introduced the concept of discrimination against disabled people in relation to employment. It provides protection and extensive employment rights for disabled people.

Governing Bodies have a duty to avoid discrimination and to make reasonable adjustments in relation to disabled employees, including those who become disabled, or whose condition worsens. Under the DDA, a Governing Body has a positive duty to retain disabled employees wherever it is reasonable to do so.

The DfEE has issued a circular to schools, *What the Disability Discrimination Act means for schools and LEAs* (3/97), relevant extracts of which are given here, though schools should be aware of the full version. The Act also provides for detailed regulations and a statutory employment Code of Practice.

The Act's definition of disability

The definition of a disabled person under the Act is a person with:

"...a physical or mental impairment which has a substantial or long-term adverse effect on their ability to carry out normal day-to-day activities."

The definition covers:

- physical, sensory, or mental impairments, including learning disabilities;

- progressive conditions (such as cancer, multiple sclerosis, muscular dystrophy, and HIV infection) from the moment the condition leads to an impairment which affects the ability to carry out normal day-to-day activities, even if it is not a substantial effect, if the effect is likely to become substantial eventually;

- severe disfigurements;

- people who have had a disability in the past, for example someone who has suffered from a nervous breakdown and has since recovered.

The definition does not cover:

- people addicted to alcohol, nicotine, or any other substance (other than as a result of the substance being medically prescribed);

- people with seasonal allergic rhinitis (e.g. hayfever), unless it aggravates the effect of another condition;

- people with a tendency to physical or sexual abuse of others;

- tendency to set fires;

- tendency to steal;

- exhibitionism;

- voyeurism.

The meaning of discrimination

Under the DDA, 'discrimination' occurs when a disabled person is treated less favourably than someone else and:

- the treatment is for a reason relating to the person's disability which does not, or would not, apply to others, and this treatment cannot be justified;

- fails to comply with the duty to make reasonable adjustments and that failure cannot be justified.

Employing staff

Employers must not unjustifiably discriminate against current or prospective employees with disabilities, or those who have had disabilities in the past. This applies to every aspect of work, including recruitment, terms and conditions of service, promotion, training and the dismissal process.

Employers may have to make reasonable adjustments to their employment arrangements or premises if these substantially disadvantage a disabled employee compared to a non-disabled person. For prospective employees, they must investigate whether there is any reasonable adjustment which would overcome a disadvantage to a disabled applicant before deciding if they are the most suitable person for the job.

The employment provisions of the DDA apply to all existing and prospective staff, teaching and non-teaching, in schools, except staff in very small voluntary aided, foundation, or foundation special schools. This includes part-time and temporary or casual staff.

The Act does not prevent an employer from appointing the best person for the job.

Reasonable adjustments

LEAs and Governing Bodies may have to make reasonable adjustments to their employment arrangements or premises so that a disabled employee or prospective employee is not at any substantial disadvantage compared to a non-disabled person. The duty to make reasonable adjustments applies in respect of individual disabled employees or job applicants. There is no requirement to make adjustments in anticipation of ever having a disabled employee.

Many adjustments which it is reasonable for the Governing Body to make will have no or minimal cost. Governing Bodies of LEA schools should discuss individual cases with their LEA. Advice is also available from the Employment Service through its Disability Service Teams.

Examples of reasonable adjustments
Adjustments may need to be considered in any respect of the disabled person's job, including working conditions, accommodation, and training and development.

For prospective employees, adjustments may need to be made to the job application process, including advertising, the selection criteria, the ways in which candidates are assessed, interview arrangements, or when making the job offer.

There are no fixed rules about the number of types of adjustments which should be made for each disabled employee or prospective employee. It is important to consider each case carefully in the light of the individual's needs. Governing Bodies should think widely and positively about the type of adjustments which may be made.

A checklist of possible reasonable adjustments

The following adjustments should be considered:

- altering premises, e.g. widening a doorway, providing a ramp, stair-climbing chairs or non-slip flooring, moving classroom or corridor furniture, altering lighting, or providing parking spaces for disabled drivers;

- allocating some duties to another employee, such as asking a non-disabled teacher to assemble a slide projector and screen for a disabled teacher, or arranging supervision duty rosters to take account of mobility, e.g. library supervision may be more appropriate than playground supervision for a disabled teacher;

- transferring the person to fill an existing vacancy, e.g. if a teacher becomes disabled and there is no reasonable adjustment which can enable them to continue in their post, they might be considered for another suitable teaching post. In LEA-maintained schools, the LEA may be able to recommend the teacher for a suitable vacancy at another school;

- altering working hours, e.g. allowing an employee who becomes disabled to work part-time or to job share, or making adjustments to the timetable;

- changing the person's place of work, e.g. ensuring that a teacher with mobility difficulties can teach all lessons in classrooms on the ground floor;

- allowing absences during working hours for rehabilitation, assessment or treatment;

- supplying additional training, e.g. training in the use of particular pieces of equipment unique to the disabled person or re-training a teacher in a new subject area in order for them to continue teaching;
- acquiring or making changes to equipment, e.g. providing an induction loop in the school hall and other assembly areas, providing magnifying facilities, a pager that vibrates, a visible fire alarm system, or an adapted telephone;
- providing a reader or signer, e.g. reading information to a visually impaired person at particular times during the working day.

Circumstances in which less favourable treatment is justified

If a disabled job applicant is not suitable for the job for reasons related to their disability (for example, the applicant has a serious mental illness and may place pupils or other staff at risk) and no reasonable adjustment can remove that risk or make it acceptable or practicable, the Governing Body would not have to appoint that person.

No-one who is medically unfit to teach, and for whom a reasonable adjustment cannot be made, should be employed as a teacher. The health, education and welfare of pupils are of paramount importance in reaching a decision on an individual's fitness to teach. There is nothing in the DDA to prevent LEAs and Governing Bodies from refusing to employ, or continuing to employ, staff who are medically unfit to teach, including those with personality disorders. Certain conditions, such as the tendency to physical or sexual abuse of others, are explicitly excluded from the DDA.

Circumstances in which adjustments are not required

Governing Bodies and LEAs are only required to make adjustments where it is reasonable to have to do so. This depends on all the circumstances of the case. Governing Bodies and LEAs will not be required to make adjustments:

- if the disabled person only experiences a minor disadvantage. Governing Bodies and LEAs should consult disabled employees about the implications of their disability for their work;

- if they do not know that a person has a disability (and it is reasonable that they do not know), Governing Bodies should ask their employees if they have a disability which affects their work in order to consider appropriate adjustments.

In deciding whether an adjustment is 'reasonable', employment tribunals will consider the following factors:

- how much an alteration will improve the situation for the disabled employee or prospective employee;
- how easy it is to make the adjustment;
- the cost of the adjustment, both financially and in terms of disruption;
- the extent of the employer's financial or other resources. For LEA-maintained schools, this is the local authority's resources. For voluntary aided and foundation schools, this is the Governing Body's resources;
- financial or other help that may be available. For example, financial assistance may be available from a government programme such as Access to Work.

Access to Work is run by the Employment Service and can help with additional costs, for example additional fares to work, special equipment, and adaptations to equipment and buildings. Contact them via the local job centre.

Prospective employees

Governing Bodies and LEAs must not discriminate against disabled people in:

- job advertisements;
- the application process;
- the selection criteria used;
- the interview procedure;
- the terms of employment offered;
- deliberately not offering a disabled person the job.

Job advertisements and application forms

Advertisements and application forms may, as part of an equal opportunities statement, invite disabled people to apply. If the school's application form asks whether the applicant is disabled, then great care should be taken to ensure that this information is not used improperly, i.e. as a means of 'weeding out' disabled candidates. Information about jobs may need to be offered in an alternative format, e.g. via minicom or in Braille. It is important to ensure that selection criteria are not applied in a way which is discriminatory.

The interview

If the Governing Body invites a person they know to be disabled for interview, they may need to make reasonable adjustments so that the disabled person is not at a disadvantage.

If the job applicant has mobility difficulties, it may be a reasonable adjustment to allow more time to look around the school. If the applicant uses a wheelchair, it may be a reasonable adjustment for the Governing Body to use a room for the interview that is physically accessible to the applicant. If the job applicant is hearing impaired, it may be a reasonable adjustment to provide a sign language interpreter or lip speaker for them.

Selection panels should discuss the effects of the disability with the applicant and consult them about what reasonable adjustments might be necessary if the applicant were appointed. However, the emphasis should be on the applicant's skills and abilities for the post.

The job offer

Governing Bodies and LEAs must not unjustifiably refuse to employ a disabled person because of their disability. However, if, having considered what reasonable adjustments may be made, a disabled person would not be the best person for the job, the Governing Body would not have to appoint that person.

Positive action in favour of disabled people

Governing Bodies and LEAs are not required to treat a disabled person more favourably than others (although the DDA does not prohibit positive action in favour of disabled people). Governing Bodies and LEAs may wish to include in their equal opportunities policies the good practice of guaranteeing an interview to all suitably qualified disabled applicants.

Governing Bodies must not discriminate against existing disabled employees in any aspect of their employment, including:

- terms and conditions of employment;
- opportunities for promotion;
- career development or training;
- dismissal proceedings.

If an existing employee becomes disabled or an employee has a disability which worsens, the Governing Body should consult the person about their needs and, if the employee has a progressive condition, what effect that may have on future employment.

The Governing Body will need to consider making reasonable adjustments for the disabled person.

It may be a reasonable adjustment to hold a job open for someone whilst they take time off to recuperate. It may be that as a result of a disability it becomes very difficult for an employee to continue working at a particular LEA school. The LEA may be able to recommend the teacher to the Governing Body of a school in the LEA with better physical access or other facilities which at the time has a vacancy. It would be for that Governing Body to judge whether the teacher was the right person for the vacancy.

Governing Bodies and LEAs should take account of the possibility of remission in some conditions which can last for years and during which time the individual is able to continue working without difficulty.

Dismissal proceedings

If a Governing Body decides to dismiss a disabled employee for a reason relating to their disability, they would need to justify their decision. The reason for the dismissal would have to be one which could not be removed by any reasonable adjustment.

It would be justifiable to terminate the employment of a teacher with a worsening progressive condition if it became unreasonable for the Governing Body or LEA to make the degree of adjustment necessary.

Costs and compensation awarded by employment tribunals

Section 57 of the School Standards and Framework Act 1998 (SSFA) specifies that costs associated with dismissals shall not be deducted, in full or in part, from the delegated budgets of LEA maintained schools unless the LEA has good reason. These costs include legal costs and compensation awarded by employment tribunals. An example of a good reason might be that an LEA had advised a Governing Body that dismissing a disabled employee was likely to be judged unfair by an employment tribunal and the Governing Body had acted against that advice, or that the Governing Body had acted without seeking advice from the LEA.

The SSFA does not specify arrangements for employment tribunal awards in cases which do not involve dismissal, premature retirement or voluntary severance. So, for example, it does not deal with costs awarded in cases brought under the DDA of discrimination against disabled applicants.

The Governing Bodies of foundation schools may have to pay any costs or compensation themselves and should, therefore, make sure that they have the appropriate legal expenses insurance cover.

Support from Disability Service Teams

The DfEE offers help for disabled employees through Disability Service Teams. The aim is to help new and existing employees overcome some of the practical problems of disability, mainly through their Access to Work Scheme. This can be through advice and/or financial assistance.

Financial assistance may be provided to buy special aids and equipment for an employee to enable him/her to pursue their work with greater ease. There is also the possibility of providing a support worker, for example to provide readers for those employees with visual impairments.

Good practice

Good practice will ensure that the school promotes a positive attitude towards disabled persons. This will not only assist disabled employees and prospective employees but also provide protection for the school against alleged breaches of the DDA. Employers who follow an equal opportunities policy which covers disability are likely be looked on favourably by a tribunal.

A checklist for having regard to the DDA

Senior managers and Governing Bodies should:

- review all key employment policies and procedures (e.g. equal opportunities, recruitment, grievance) to ensure that the school is aware of the implications of DDA;
- make available training to those staff and governors likely to deal with employment issues, particularly recruitment;
- consult staff, professional associations and trade unions to increase awareness and to encourage co-operation and support for the school's policies and their implementation.

APPENDIX A

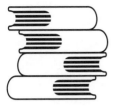

A MODEL STAFF COUNSELLING SCHEME

Staff Counselling Scheme for .... School

The Governing Body recognises that the well-being of all staff has a direct impact on the quality of teaching and learning and the effective functioning of the school. It is expected that managers will exercise the basic skills of listening and counselling so that they are able to offer help to the staff they manage. The school INSET plan will address the need to provide training to enable managers and other staff to watch for signs of stress and deal with it appropriately.

The Governing Body recognises that there will be occasions when members of staff may feel in need of professional counselling about work-related or personal issues which require expertise beyond the managerial support described above. In this case, an employee may be offered up to six one-hour sessions with a qualified counsellor. It is important to note that the counsellors do not offer cures or solutions to life-long problems. They are not a replacement for medical or psychiatric help but they may be able to suggest a way forward to help clients reach a decision or sort out a problem that will not go away. They are never a substitute for managerial responsibility.

Confidentiality between counsellor and the individual client is absolute. The only exception to this strict rule will occur if any issue involving child protection arises during the course of counselling. A request for counselling should be made to .... who will authorise the use of the scheme provided that s/he is satisfied that, where appropriate, the support available from within the school has been accessed. If agreement to use the scheme is given, the member of staff will be given the telephone number of the counselling service and is then at liberty to contact any of the counsellors listed to make an appointment.

The school will be informed by the counsellor of the name of the member of staff and the times and dates of the counselling sessions, which will normally be outside time-tabled time. The content of the counselling is strictly confidential between the employee and the counsellor and will not be reported back to the school unless child protection issues are involved. If the employee wishes to have more than six sessions, the cost will normally be borne by the employee. This employee benefit is available to all staff after the completion one year's service with the school. Part-time employees are entitled to the benefit on a pro-rata basis.

APPENDIX B

A MODEL POLICY FOR HEALTH PROMOTION

Health Promotion Policy for .... School

The Governing Body recognises and fully accepts responsibility as (or acting on behalf of) the employer for the health, safety and welfare of staff employed by the Governing Body to work at the school. The Governing Body, within the limits of resources available to it, will actively promote ways in which the health of staff can be monitored and sustained or improved. The governors are of the view that ill-health, due to whatever cause, is a misfortune which can occur to anyone at any time and for any reason. Ill-health therefore requires proactive supportive management techniques in order, as far as is reasonably possible, to minimise the personal and organisational consequences of ill-health. This health promotion policy, therefore, is complementary to the school's health and safety policy.

Recruitment and selection

The full range of tasks and demands of the job will be set out clearly in the job description sent to all candidates and will be fully discussed in the interview process. Areas of potential pressure will, as far as possible, be identified. Referees will be asked for information on candidates' sickness and absence records. Candidates' resilience and tolerance to stress will be a factor to be considered in the interview process.

The Governing Body will comply with the letter and spirit of the Disability Discrimination Act 1995.

Pre-employment health screening will be carried out prior to appointment. The process will be used in a positive way to ensure that new employees are matched to the requirements of jobs and to tailor the induction process so that the job can be performed most effectively.

Induction and promotion

All employees will receive an induction programme when they begin a new job. An evaluation will take place at the end of the induction period to identify further training requirements. As part of the induction programme, the Health Policy will be discussed.

Absence management

As part of line management responsibility, sickness absences will be discussed with the employee shortly after the member of staff returns to work. Where the absence has been as a result of stress or causes which the individual believes are work-related, then the line manager will discuss that with the member of staff and make all reasonable efforts to minimise a recurrence. The line manager will also inform............ that the employee believes that the cause of the absence is work-related.

The line manager will arrange to talk with, or visit, any absent colleague within five working days of the first day of absence to discuss any underlying causes and to arrange support and assistance if the absence is likely to continue. Where the employee's medical adviser advises that it would be beneficial for the member of staff to return to work on a 'therapeutic basis' i.e. technically remaining on sick leave but attending work, normally part-time, under the direct supervision of another member of staff and without job responsibility, then this will be considered. Under these circumstances, the employee will be asked to give consent to examination by the school's medical adviser to ensure that this is an appropriate course of action for the employer to take.

Training and development

The Governing Body recognises that changed or changing job requirements are significant stress-inducing factors and therefore has a policy of identifying staff training needs, in line with the school improvement plan.

APPENDIX C

A MODEL POLICY FOR NOTIFYING SICKNESS ABSENCE

1. Notification of Sickness Absence

1.1   An employee in a school who is prevented by illness from reporting for duty shall notify the headteacher as soon as possible by note or telephone on the FIRST DAY OF ABSENCE.

1.2   A doctor's certificate must be provided from the eighth day of absence (including Saturdays and Sundays) and at appropriate intervals, according to Conditions of Service, for the purposes of claiming DSS benefit and sickness allowance under sickness pay conditions of service.

1.3   In cases where the doctor's first statement covers a period exceeding fourteen days or where more than one statement is necessary, the employee must, before returning to work, obtain a final statement as to fitness to resume duties.

1.4   Absence on account of sickness on the day before or day following a public or extra-statutory holiday must be supported by a self-certificate.

2. Sickness Absence - Self-Certification

2.1   All employees must complete a self-certification form detailing the reason for absence for any period of sickness absence up to seven days and for the first seven days of any longer absence unless covered by a medical certificate. The self-certification form must be completed immediately on return to duty.

2.2   Support (former Manual) staff are required to submit self-certification forms for all periods of absence and Support (former APT&C) staff and teachers must identify the reason for absence on the fourth working day of absence where the absence lasted beyond three days, in accordance with Conditions of Service requirements.

3. Medical Examination during Period of Absence

3.1   An employee shall, if required at any time, submit to a medical examination by a registered medical practitioner nominated by the employer, subject to the provisions of the Access to Medical Reports Act 1988 where applicable. In the event of a difference in medical opinion as to the employee's fitness for work, the matter shall, at the request of the employer or of the employee, be submitted to an independent medical referee chosen jointly by the employer and the employee.

4. Reimbursement of Cost of Doctors' Statements

4.1   Where the Governors require a doctor's statement from an employee, the employer shall, on provision of a receipt, reimburse the employee if a charge is made for the statement.

5. Illness or Injury arising from Work

5.1   Any accident arising out of and in the course of employment with the employer must be reported and recorded in accordance with the procedures laid down by the employer. The accident will be subject to investigation and report by an employee authorised for the purpose by the employer.

5.2   Where an employee seeks medical advice about an illness which is suspected or alleged to result from the nature of his or her employment, the employee must report relevant information to the headteacher at the first opportunity.

5.3   In the case of the first and any subsequent absence due to industrial disease or accident, an employee shall submit, at any time during such absence, if so required by the employer, to a medical examination by a registered medical practitioner nominated by the employer. In the event that the employer's doctor is not satisfied that the absence is due to an industrial disease or accident, the employee shall have right of appeal to an independent medical referee chosen jointly by the employer and the employee.

6. False Information

6.1.   The provision of any false information could result in disciplinary action being taken, including the possibility of dismissal.

APPENDIX D
A MODEL FORM FOR SICKNESS ABSENCE SELF-CERTIFICATION

Sickness Absence Self-Certification Form for _____ School/College

To be completed by all employees for any period of sickness absence up to seven days, unless the full period of absence is covered by a medical certificate.

1. Name   Mr/Mrs/Ms/Miss/Dr _____

2. I hereby certify that I was unable to work:

    from: _____ day _____ date (first day of absence)

    to: _____ day _____ date (last day of absence)

    because I was suffering from:

    _____

    _____

3. Was your illness due to an accident at work?   Yes/No

    Signed _____   Date _____
           employee

4   I certify that, to the best of my knowledge, this certificate has been completed by the employee and that the employee was absent from work for the period shown.

    Signed _____   Date _____
           headteacher

Notes
1. Employees are required to notify the headteacher of absence due to sickness by 8.30 a.m. on the first day of absence.
2. If unable to return to work on the fourth day of absence, an employee must further notify the headteacher, giving information as to the nature and probable duration of illness.
3. A doctor's certificate must be obtained for a period of illness lasting more than seven days (including Saturday and Sunday) and should be forwarded to the headteacher not later than the eighth day of absence.
4. Upon returning to work, all employees must complete and sign the Authority's Sickness Absence Self-Certification form for any period up to the first seven days of absence through illness or injury, which is not covered by a medical-certificate.
    (Note: conditions of service for manual workers require a self-certificate for all days of absence up to and including the seventh day. Teachers and APT&C staff are required by their conditions of service to provide a certificate from the fourth working day of absence.)
5. An accident report must be completed where absence was due to an injury sustained at work.
6 . Provision of any false information regarding an employee's absence will be treated as gross misconduct and could lead to dismissal.

APPENDIX E
FURTHER READING

ACAS — Health and Employment, Advisory Booklet No.15, 1990.

Bernard, M. — Taking the Stress out of Teaching, Collins, 1990.

Earnshaw, J. — Stress and Employer Liability, Institute of Personnel and Development, 1996.

Evans, A. and Palmer, S. — From Absence to Attendance, Institute of Personnel and Development, 1997.

Health and Safety Executive — Managing Occupational Stress: a Guide for Managers and Teachers in the Schools Sector, HSE Books.

Incomes Data Services — Absence and Sick Pay Policies Study 556, June 1994.

The Industrial Society — Managing Best Practice: Maximising Attendance, The Industrial Society, 1997.

Johnson, M. — Stress in Teaching: an overview of Research, SCRE Publication 103, 1989.

Robertson, J. — Effective Classroom Control: Understanding Teacher-Pupil Relationships, Hodder and Stoughton, London, 2nd Edition.

Rogers, B. — Supporting Teachers in the Workplace, Jacaranda Press, Milton Queensland, 1992.

Rogers, B. — The Language of Discipline: a Practical Approach to Effective Classroom Management, Northcote House Publishers Ltd, 2nd Edition, 1997.

Swain, M. — How to Deal with Sickness and Absence, Gee Publishing, 1995.

APPENDIX F
USEFUL ADDRESSES

Association of Counselling at Work
BAC
1 Regent Place
Rugby CV21 2PJ
Tel: 01788 578328
website: www.counselling.co.uk

Education Personnel
Management Ltd
St John's House
Spitfire Close
Ermine Business Park
Huntingdon
Cambs. PE18 6EP
Tel: 01480 431993
Fax: 01480 431992
website: www.epm.co.uk
e-mail: epm@educ-personnel.co.uk

Health and Safety Executive
HSE Information Centre
Broad Lane
Sheffield
S3 7HQ
HSE Infoline Tel: 0541 545500
website: www.hse.gov.uk

The Industrial Society
Robert Hyde House
48 Bryanston Square
London W1H 7LN
Tel: 020 7479 2000
website: www.indsoc.gov.uk

Institute of Personnel and
Development
IPD House
35 Camp Road
London SW19 4UX
Tel: 020 8971 9000 (ask for enquiries)
website: www.ipd.co.uk (accessible to
non-members)

The Employers Organisation for
Local Governments (Formerly the
Local Government Management Board)
Layden House
76-86 Turnmill Street
London EC1M 5LG
Tel: 020 7296 6600
website www.lg-employers.gov.uk

Society of Occupational Medicine
6 St Andrews Place
Regents Park
London
NW1 4LB
Tel: 020 7486 2641
website: www.som.org.uk

National Healthy School Standard
Health Development Agency
Trevelyan House
30 Great Peter Street
London
SW1P 2HW
Tel: 020 7431 1865
website: www.wiredforhealth.gov.uk

EDUCATION PERSONNEL MANAGEMENT SERIES

MANAGING CHALLENGING PEOPLE
dealing with staff conduct

by Maureen Cooper and Bev Curtis
ISBN: 1-85539-057-4

This handbook deals with managing staff whose conduct gives cause for concern. It summarises the employment relationships in schools and those areas of education and employment law relevant to staff discipline. It looks at the difference between conduct and capability, and misconduct and gross misconduct, and describes disciplinary and dimissal procedures relating to teaching and non-teaching staff and headteachers.

MANAGING POOR PERFORMANCE
handling staff capability issues

by Maureen Cooper and Bev Curtis
ISBN: 1-85539-062-0

This handbook explains clearly why capability is important, and gives advice on how to identify staff with poor performance and how to help them improve. It outlines the legal position and the role of governors, and details the various stages of formal capability procedures and dismissal hearings. The book provides model letters to use and is illustrated by real-life case studies. This provides the help you need to give you confidence in tackling these difficult issues.